Animals Can Be Superheroes!

Have you ever wanted to be a superhero and help others using your superpowers? Did you know that both wild animals and pets have used their skills to take care of others? Read this book to find out which animal helpers have come to the rescue by using their super skills.

Contents

www.capstonepub.com
Visit our website to find out more information about Heinemann-Raintree books.

To order:
☎ Phone 800-747-4992
💻 Visit www.capstonepub.com
  to browse our catalog and order online.

Edited by Rebecca Rissman, Dan Nunn,
  and Catherine Veitch
Designed by Joanna Hinton-Malivoire
Picture research by Mica Brancic
Production by Victoria Fitzgerald

Originated by Capstone Global Library
Printed and bound in China by CTPS

16 15 14 13 12
10 9 8 7 6 5 4 3 2 1

Library of Congress Cataloging-in-Publication Data
Townsend, John
Amazing animal helpers / John Townsend.—1st ed.
p. cm.—(Animal superpowers)
Includes bibliographical references and index.
ISBN 978-1-4109-4745-1 (hb)
ISBN 978-1-4109-4752-9 (pb) 1. Pets—Behavior. I. Title.
SF412.5.T69 2013
636.088'7—dc23
        2011041354

Acknowledgments
We would like to thank the following for permission to reproduce photographs: Alamy p. 14 (© Asia–RM); Corbis pp. 11 (epa/© WEDA), 19 (Sygma/© Jeremy Bembaron), 29 (dpa/© Rolf Haid); Getty Images pp. 5 (FEMA/Mike Rieger), 15 (Dan Kitwood), 25 (AFP Photo/ Carl Court); iStockphoto p. 4 (© Seon Winn); Mary Evans Picture Library p. 22 (© Metropolitan Police Authority); Press Association p. 17 (Yao tingshan/AP); Rex Features p. 24 (Gordon Agg Jones); Shutterstock pp. 6 (© ShopArtGallery), 7 (© Jim Agronick), 8 (© Waldemar Dabrowski), 9 (© Stephen Meese), 10 (© Ben Heys), 12 (© Tan Hung Meng), 13 (© Moomsabuy), 16 (© Luna Vandoorne), 18 (© Arvind Balaraman), 21 (© pyast), 26 (© Reddogs), 27 (© Dennis Donohue), 20 (© Niall Dunne); The Bridgeman Art Library p. 23 (© Look and Learn/Private Collection).

Cover photograph of an avalanche rescue dog, Baerli, and Bavarian Alpine rescue worker, Andreas Oeckler, January 23, 2008, reproduced with permission of Corbis (Reuters/Alexandra Beier).

Every effort has been made to contact copyright holders of material reproduced in this book. Any omissions will be rectified in subsequent printings if notice is given to the publisher.

We would like to thank Michael Bright for his invaluable help in the preparation of this book.

Disclaimer
All the Internet addresses (URLs) given in this book were valid at the time of going to press. However, due to the dynamic nature of the Internet, some addresses may have changed, or sites may have changed or ceased to exist since publication. While the author and publisher regret any inconvenience this may cause readers, no responsibility for any such changes can be accepted by either the author or the publisher.

Some words are shown in bold, **like this**. You can find out what they mean by looking in the glossary.

ANIMAL SUPERPOWERS

AMAZING ANIMAL HELPERS

John Townsend

Raintree

Chicago, Illinois

Some animals have been helpers in times of danger.

Super Rescue

Dolphins can sense when people are in danger. In 2004, a family was swimming in New Zealand when a great white shark swam at them. Suddenly, about six dolphins formed a barrier around them, to keep the shark away. When the shark gave up, the dolphins helped the swimmers back to shore.

dolphin

Super Friend

Seals are intelligent sea **mammals** with amazing skills. In 2002, a dog swimming in the Tees River, in England, was swept away downriver. Suddenly, a seal's head popped up and circled the drowning dog. Then the seal nudged the dog with its nose to push it to shore. Safe at last!

Super Warning

Elephants can pick up sounds and **vibrations** in the ground through their feet and trunks. When a **tsunami** struck Thailand in 2004, elephants seemed to know it was coming. Many moved to higher ground to escape, and they took their tourist riders with them.

Did You Know?
Elephants helped to clear up the damage caused by the tsunami.

Super Insects

Ants are mini superheroes. For their size, they are super-strong and can lift 20 times their own body weight. That's not all. Some ants act like heroes to save each other from a **predator**, even when they risk getting killed themselves.

Ants work as a team to build a bridge, so that other ants can crawl across.

Did You Know?
If food is too big to carry back to the nest, the ant gets another ant to help it carry the food.

Super Caring

Although gorillas can be **aggressive**, they can act like superheroes. In 1996, a gorilla named Binti Jua helped a three-year-old boy when he fell into her pen at a zoo near Chicago. She rushed over to comfort him. She kept him safe from other gorillas until he could be rescued.

Super Saver

Whales can be super-intelligent and caring. Mila, a beluga whale, stopped a diver from drowning in China in 2009. Yang Yun dived to the bottom of Mila's pool in "Polar Land." But bad **cramps** stopped her from returning to the surface. Mila rushed to the rescue, grabbed Yun's leg, and pushed her up to get air.

Yang Yun

Mila

17

Super Flight

Pigeons have been used to carry messages because of their skill at flying long distances and finding their way. In fog at sea in World War II, the crew of a crashed plane sent pigeons with details of where they were. After rescue came, the pigeons received special medals for their bravery.

message

Did You Know?

In wars, carrier pigeons saved lives by carrying important secret messages through gunfire.

Super Pet

Cats are not just smart. They also have super **vision** and hearing. One night in 2010, in his New Zealand home, Maceo the cat sensed danger. A neighbor's shed was on fire. Maceo dipped his paws into the toilet then walked over his owners' faces. They woke to escape, just in time.

Maceo's owners woke to see a blaze right outside their window.

Super Cool

Some horses can be super-brave. During World War II, police horses received medals for being heroes. In 1947, when bombs fell on London, England, a window smashed down in front of police horse Olga. She bolted in fear, but she returned to the scene to help with rescues.

Olga

Super Sniffer

As man's best friend, dogs are our most **loyal** animal superhero helpers. Their excellent hearing, sense of smell, and super-intelligence make many dogs real heroes during danger. Two dogs awarded medals for bravery were Endal and Treo.

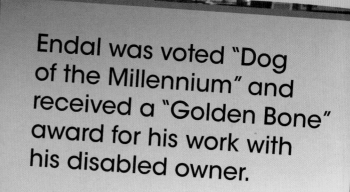

Endal was voted "Dog of the Millennium" and received a "Golden Bone" award for his work with his disabled owner.

Treo was awarded a special medal for sniffing out roadside bombs in Afghanistan.

Super Brave

A pet dog named Angel became a hero in 2010, when he stopped a mountain lion from attacking an 11-year-old boy in Canada. The boy was collecting firewood outside his home when the wild cat attacked. Angel was badly hurt, but he recovered and was praised for saving the boy's life.

Did You Know?
The mountain lion is also known as a puma or cougar.

Quiz: Spot the Superhero!

Test your powers of observation and see if you can spot the superhero. You can find the answers on page 32, if you are really stuck!

1. Which of these animals has saved people from sharks?
a) a dog
b) a dolphin
c) a seal

2. Which of these animals can hear through its feet?
a) an elephant
b) an ant
c) a whale

3. Which of these animals has worked for the police?
a) a horse
b) a gorilla
c) a cat

4. Which of these animals has won medals?
a) a shark
b) a pigeon
c) a puma

5. Which of these animals has rescued people?
a) a dog
b) an ant
c) a cougar

Glossary

aggressive unfriendly and likely to attack

cramps muscle pains

loyal faithful and reliable

mammal warm-blooded animal that makes milk for its young

predator animal that hunts other animals

tsunami great sea wave produced by an earthquake or volcano under the sea

vibration trembling movement

vision eyesight

Find Out More

Books

Bingham, Jane. *Animal Heroes* (War Stories). Chicago: Heinemann Library, 2011.

Gilpin, Daniel. *Record-Breaking Animals* (Record Breakers). New York: PowerKids, 2012.

Johnson, Jinny. *Amazing Animals* (Explorers). New York: Kingfisher, 2012.

Markle, Sandra. *Animal Heroes: True Rescue Stories.* Minneapolis, Minn.: Millbrook, 2009.

Websites

www.allaboutanimals.org.uk/index.asp
Learn all about animals on this Website.

www.bbc.co.uk/newsround/15749027
Find out about heroic horses used in battle.

Index

Answers: 1.b, 2.a, 3.a, 4.b, 5.a.